THE AUTHOR
POEMS & SONGS

THE NAMES OF CHRIST ILLUSTRATED
ACTIVITY BOOK

THE NOC ILLUSTRATED ACTIVITY BOOKS: AN AMAZING WAY TO TEACH YOUTH THE MANY DIFFERENT CHARACTERS OF CHRIST FOUND IN THE HOLY SCRIPTURES.

ISBN: 1-441-46173-6

PRINTED IN THE UNITED STATES OF AMERICA

COVER PAGE DESIGNED BY DYNAMIC ANIMATION PRODUCTIONS, LLC

PREFACE

"Looking unto Jesus the author and finisher of our faith; who for the joy that was set before him endured the cross, despising the shame, and is set down at the right hand of the throne of God." HEBREWS 12:2 (KJV)

To our parents, teachers and guardians: it is a privilege to study God's word with your children and a blessing to train and discipline them for service in the master's cause. Along with their bibles, we strongly encourage your participation in the child's usage of this activity book.

"HARMONY IN MAZES"

SEEK AND FIND YOUR WAY THROUGH THE MAZE BELOW

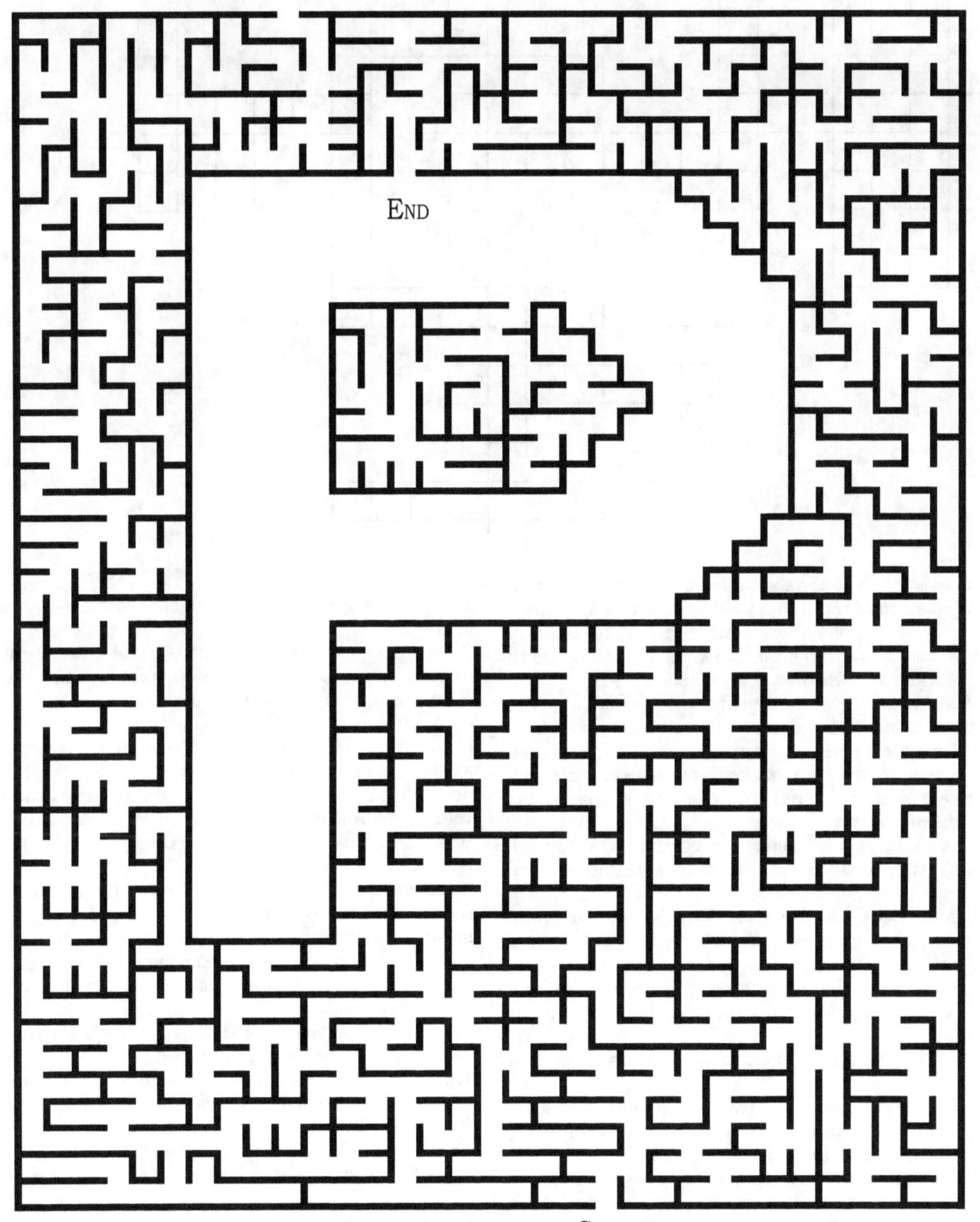

END

START

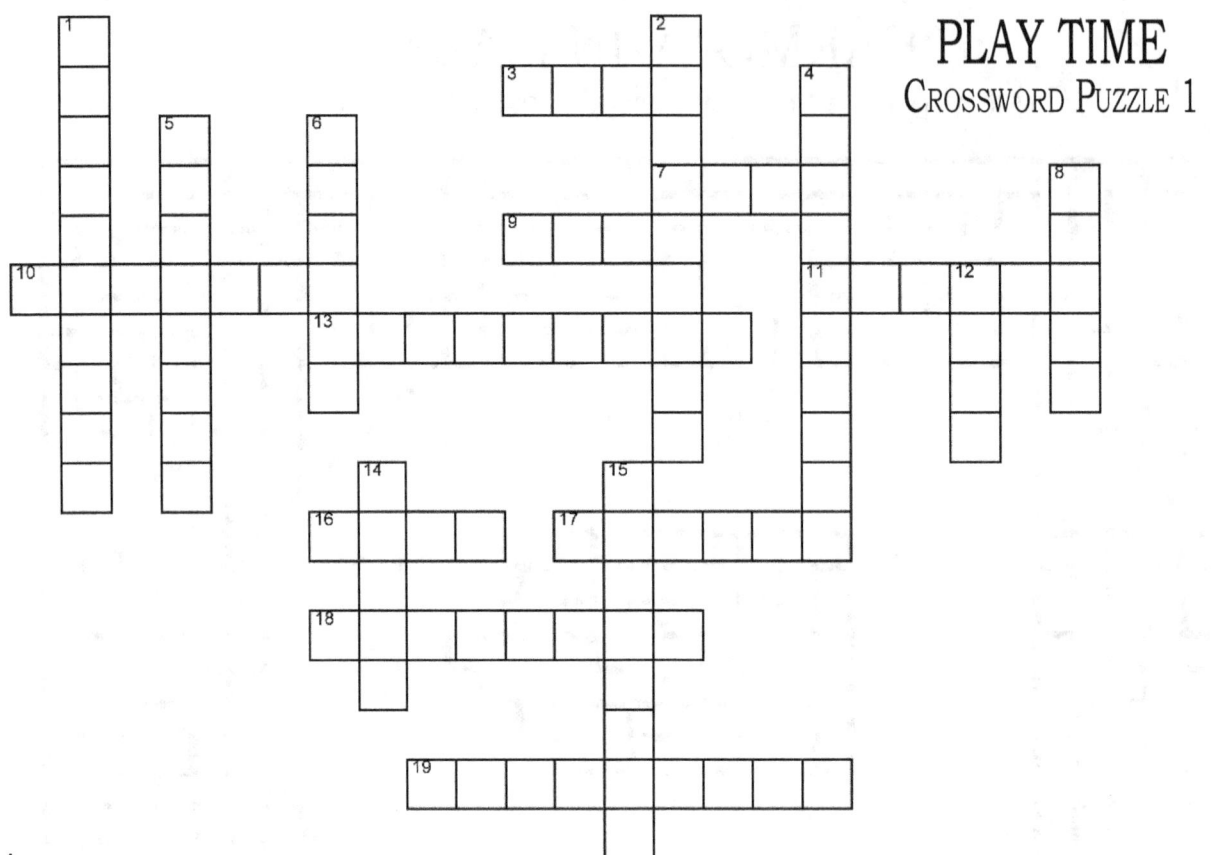

ACROSS

3. CONSISTS OF A CONCAVE MOUTHPIECE, A CONICAL TUBE WITH FOUR TO SIX PISTONS AND A BELL FACING UP WITH A WIDE SHAPE.

7. A SLENDER WOODWIND INSTRUMENT WITH A CONICAL BORE AND A DOUBLE-REED MOUTHPIECE, HAVING A RANGE OF THREE OCTAVES AND A PENETRATING, POIGNANT SOUND.

9. A STRINGED MUSICAL INSTRUMENT WITH A TRIANGULAR SHAPE, HELD UPRIGHT AND COMMONLY TOUCHED WITH THE FINGERS.

10. A SOPRANO BRASS WIND INSTRUMENT CONSISTING OF A LONG METAL TUBE LOOPED ONCE AND ENDING IN A FLARED BELL, THE MODERN TYPE BEING EQUIPPED WITH THREE VALVES FOR PRODUCING VARIATIONS IN PITCH.

11. A PERCUSSION INSTRUMENT CONSISTING OF A CONCAVE BRASS PLATE THAT MAKES A LOUD CLASHING TONE WHEN HIT WITH A DRUMSTICK OR WHEN USED IN PAIRS.

13. A PORTABLE WIND INSTRUMENT WITH A SMALL KEYBOARD AND FREE METAL REEDS THAT SOUND WHEN AIR IS FORCED PAST THEM BY PLEATED BELLOWS OPERATED BY THE PLAYER.

16. A SMALL TUBULAR WIND INSTRUMENT, SUCH AS A FLUTE, WITH HOLES AND STOPS THAT IS PLAYED BY BLOWING WITH THE MOUTH.

17. THE SMALLEST OF THE STRINGED INSTRUMENTS PLAYED WITH A BOW.

18. A WOODWIND INSTRUMENT HAVING A STRAIGHT CYLINDRICAL TUBE WITH A FLARING BELL AND A SINGLE-REED MOUTHPIECE, PLAYED BY MEANS OF FINGER HOLES AND KEYS.

19. A SMALL RECTANGULAR INSTRUMENT CONSISTING OF A ROW OF FREE REEDS SET BACK IN AIR HOLES, PLAYED BY EXHALING OR INHALING. ALSO CALLED MOUTH HARP, MOUTH ORGAN.

DOWN

1. A KIND OF ACCORDION THAT HAS BUTTONS INSTEAD OF A KEYBOARD.

2. A WOODWIND INSTRUMENT WITH A SINGLE-REED MOUTHPIECE AND A USUALLY CURVED CONICAL METAL TUBE, INCLUDING SOPRANO, ALTO, TENOR, AND BARITONE SIZES.

4. A VALVED BRASS WIND INSTRUMENT THAT PRODUCES A MELLOW TONE FROM A LONG NARROW TUBE THAT IS COILED IN A CIRCLE BEFORE ENDING IN A FLARING BELL.

5. A BRASS INSTRUMENT CONSISTING OF A LONG CYLINDRICAL TUBE BENT UPON ITSELF TWICE, ENDING IN A BELL-SHAPED MOUTH, AND HAVING A MOVABLE U-SHAPED SLIDE FOR PRODUCING DIFFERENT PITCHES.

6. A MUSICAL INSTRUMENT HAVING A LARGE FLAT-BACKED SOUND BOX, A LONG FRETTED NECK, AND USUALLY SIX STRINGS, PLAYED BY STRUMMING OR PLUCKING.

8. A FOUR-STRINGED MUSICAL INSTRUMENT OF THE VIOLIN FAMILY, PITCHED LOWER THAN THE VIOLA BUT HIGHER THAN THE DOUBLE BASS.

12. A LARGE BOWED STRING INSTRUMENT. THE LOWEST PITCHED INSTRUMENT OF THE VIOLIN FAMILY.

14. A STRINGED INSTRUMENT OF THE VIOLIN FAMILY, SLIGHTLY LARGER THAN A VIOLIN, AND HAVING A DEEPER, MORE SONOROUS TONE.

15. ONE WHO GOES BEFORE OR ACCOMPANIES, A LEADER, A CHIEF, A GUIDE. THE CONDUCTOR OF AN ORCHESTRA OR CHORUS.

CROSSWORD PUZZLE 1: ANSWERS FOUND ON PAGE 35

FILL IN THE BLANK
COMMIT THESE VERSES OF SCRIPTURE TO MEMORY

FOR HIS _____ KINDNESS IS _____ TOWARD US: AND THE _____ OF THE LORD _____ FOR EVER. PRAISE YE THE LORD. ~ PSALM 117:2

THE LORD IS MY _____ AND MY _____; MY HEART _____ IN HIM, AND I AM _____: THEREFORE MY _____ GREATLY _____; AND WITH MY _____ WILL I PRAISE HIM. ~ PSALM 28:7

I WILL _____ THE NAME OF _____ WITH A _____, AND WILL _____ HIM WITH THANKS-GIVING. ~ PSALM 69:30

AND, LO, _____ ART UNTO _____ AS A VERY _____ SONG OF ONE THAT HATH A _____ VOICE, AND CAN _____ WELL ON AN _____: FOR THEY _____ THY WORDS, BUT THEY _____ THEM NOT. ~ EZEKIEL 33:32

MY HELP _____ FROM THE LORD, WHICH MADE _____ AND _____. ~ PSALM 121:2

NOW THEREFORE _____ YE THIS _____ FOR YOU, AND _____ IT THE _____ OF ISRAEL: PUT IT IN THEIR _____, THAT THIS _____ MAY BE A _____ FOR ME _____ THE CHILDREN OF ISRAEL. ~ DEUTERONOMY 31:19

O MY _____, THOU HAST SAID UNTO THE _____, THOU ART MY LORD: MY _____ EXTEND-ETH NOT TO _____. ~ PSALM 16:2

THY _____ IS A _____ UNTO MY _____, AND A _____ UNTO MY _____. ~ PSALM 119:105

SERVE THE LORD WITH _____: _____ BEFORE HIS _____ WITH _____. ~ PSALM 100:2

I WILL NOT BE _____ OF TEN THOUSANDS OF _____, THAT HAVE _____ THEMSELVES _____ ME _____ ABOUT. ~ PSALM 3:6

THE LORD IS MY _____, AND MY _____, AND MY _____; MY GOD, MY _____, IN WHOM I WILL _____; MY _____, AND THE _____ OF MY _____, AND MY HIGH _____. ~ PSALM 18:2

AS THE _____ PANTETH AFTER THE WATER _____, SO _____ MY _____ AFTER THEE, O GOD. ~ PSALM 42:1

SEE HOW MANY WORDS
YOU CAN RHYME WITH
GRACE

"PRAISE THE LORD WITH HARP: SING UNTO HIM WITH THE PSALTERY
AND AN INSTRUMENT OF TEN STRINGS." ~ PSALM 33:2

_____

_____

_____   _____

_____   _____

_____   _____

_____   _____

SCRIPTURE SONGS 4 LEARNING

WHATSOEVER IS BORN OF GOD OVERCOMETH THE
WORLD.
WHATSOEVER IS BORN OF GOD OVERCOMETH THE
WORLD:
AND THIS IS THE VICTORY THAT OVERCOMETH THE
WORLD,
EVEN OUR FAITH, EVEN OUR FAITH.
(REPEAT)

1 JOHN 5:4

"MAKE A JOYFUL NOISE UNTO THE LORD"

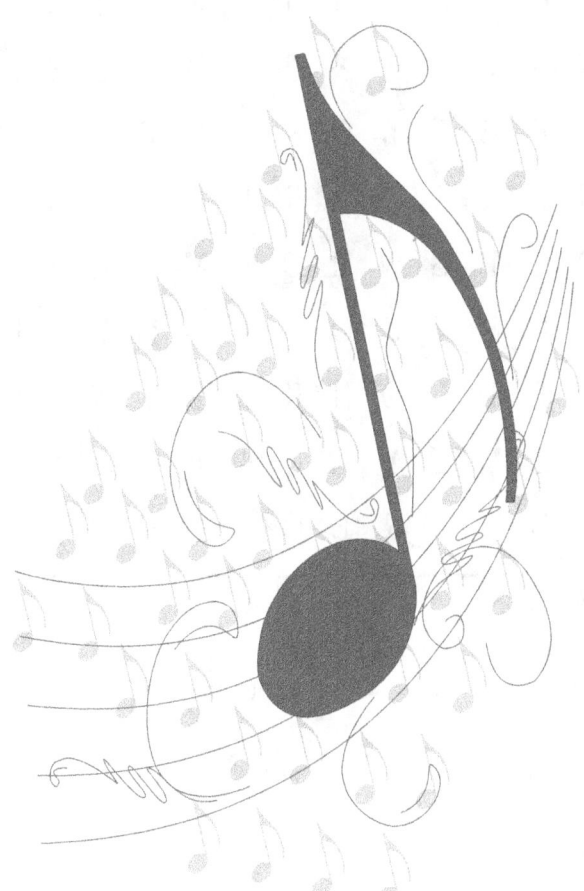

BEHOLD, THE TABERNACLE OF GOD IS WITH
MEN,
AND HE WILL DWELL WITH THEM,
AND THEY SHALL BE HIS PEOPLE,
AND GOD HIMSELF SHALL BE WITH THEM,
AND BE THEIR GOD.

AND GOD SHALL WIPE AWAY ALL TEARS FROM
THEIR EYES; AND THERE SHALL BE NO MORE
DEATH,
NEITHER SORROW, NOR CRYING,
NEITHER SHALL THERE BE ANY MORE PAIN:
FOR THE FORMER THINGS ARE PASSED AWAY.
FOR THE FORMER THINGS ARE PASSED AWAY.

REVELATION 21:3, 4

LET'S PLAY

FIND THESE WORDS IN THE FOREST OF LETTERS

```
V I O L A M N B V Q L E V H J Z U I A R K H C D N
P A Z H J V A I L R T R O M B O N E A F D S V R E
A I Z H T I Y A A C A E I M V R O V C P O A O Q V
S W U C J H C T A C W V B A S S L X X N B H V Y W
T E N J X Z I L I J U P G E X H C W I U H F V T L
I B B Z R U L N A D V I C L Z A C T T C B I K W F
L M W O G L O W A R N P O Y W E R N N U D G U E X
N X A L B M Z I C X I E L T M E S E S F T Q Y S X
P H K S R O J V C X U N U H C B R W A J R R A T I
E K Y A D E E I O Z O X E N S F A N X T U F E M W
E V H K M M L O R W R E O T R B L L O K M Q D Y S
W Z D W M C V L D O S C Y N H A R P P R P A S W Y
V G K M I M N I I I S G K D G P G W H Q E M X B L
B Z Y J P J M N O Z U J F T B S Y C O H T Q M U N
Z B A J V H X O N S C Q T C E L L O N K W L S N H
G J Z X J T H S U G Z U I L Z M E Y E Q W F X Y Q
G A L V G Y R D U R V L K X B D I R E C T O R Q Y
```

VIOLIN	OBOE	TRUMPET	BASS
VIOLA	CYMBAL	CONCERTINO	ACCORDION
HARMONICA	SAXOPHONE	TROMBONE	CLARINET
TUBA	DIRECTOR	PIPE	FRENCH HORN
HARP	GUITAR	CELLO	

WORD SEARCH 1: ANSWERS FOUND ON PAGE 36

BIBLE TRIVIA 1: "PSALMS"

1. WHERE WOULD YOU FIND THIS VERSE OF SCRIPTURE? "MY HELP COMETH FROM THE LORD, WHICH MADE HEAVEN AND EARTH".
   A) PSALM 119　　　　B) PSALM 121　　　　C) PSALM 117　　　　D) PSALM 1

2. WHERE WOULD YOU FIND THIS VERSE OF SCRIPTURE? "AS THE HART PANTETH AFTER THE WATER BROOKS, SO PANTETH MY SOUL AFTER THEE, O GOD".
   A) PSALM 41:1　　　　B) PSALM 42:1　　　　C) PSALM 44:9　　　　D) PSALM 117:2

3. WHICH OF THE FOLLOWING WAS NOT KNOWN AS A WRITER OF A PSALM?
   A) MOSES　　　　B) SOLOMON　　　　C) ALL OF THESE　　　　D) ABRAHAM

4. SELAH APPEARS 71 TIMES IN THE PSALMS, YET THE MEANING IS UNCLEAR.
   A) TRUE　　　　B) FALSE

5. WHICH TWO PSALMS DID DAVID WRITE DURING ABSALOM'S REBELLION?
   A) 34 AND 56　　　　B) 18 AND 51　　　　C) 142 AND 57　　　　D) 3 AND 7

6. WHAT IS THE SHORTEST PSALM?
   A) PSALM 134　　　　B) PSALM 117　　　　C) PSALM 119　　　　D) PSALM 133

7. WHICH OF THESE VERSES DOES NOT MENTION THE MESSIAH?
   A) PSALM 16:2　　　　B) PSALM 2:7　　　　C) PSALM 16:8-10　　　　D) PSALM 34:20

8. THE TWENTY-THIRD PSALM WAS WRITTEN BY SOLOMON.
   A) TRUE　　　　B) FALSE

9. IN WHICH PSALM WOULD YOU FIND THIS VERSE: "THY WORD IS A LAMP UNTO MY FEET AND A LIGHT UNTO MY PATH"?
   A) PSALM 121　　　　B) PSALM 118　　　　C) PSALM 117　　　　D) PSALM 119

10. THE PSALMISTS OFTEN DEMANDED GOD'S JUSTICE AND VENGEANCE AGAINST AN ENEMY.
    A) TRUE　　　　B) FALSE

11. IN WHAT PSALM WOULD YOU FIND THE FOLLOWING VERSES: "I WILL LOVE THEE, O LORD, MY STRENGTH. THE LORD IS MY ROCK, AND MY FORTRESS, AND MY DELIVERER; MY GOD, MY STRENGTH, IN WHOM I WILL TRUST; MY BUCKLER, AND THE HORN OF MY SALVATION, AND MY HIGH TOWER".
    A) PSALM 16:5-6　　　　B) PSALM 18:1-2　　　　C) PSALM 121:1-2　　　　D) PSALM 37:39-40

12. HOW MANY PSALMS ARE THERE?
    ANSWER:

BIBLE TRIVIA 1: ANSWERS FOUND ON PAGE 34

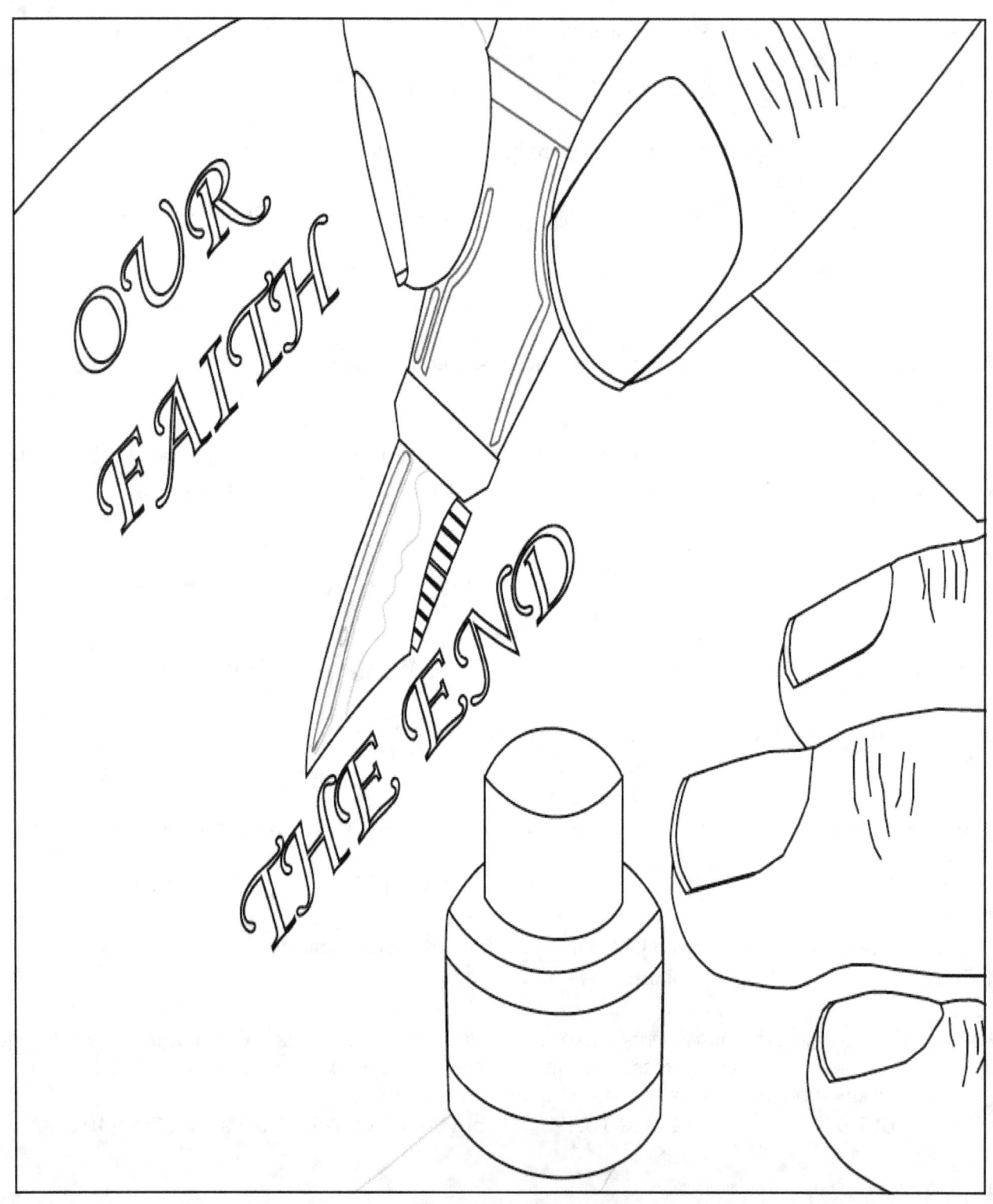

THE AUTHOR

LONG AGO IN OLD JUDEA
CAME THE SICK, THE BLIND, THE LAME,
TO THE FAR FAMED HEALING FOUNTAIN
WHERE THE ANGEL FOOTSTEPS CAME
HOW THEY WATCHED, SO SAD AND LONELY,
FOR THE TROUBLING OF THE POOL,
WHEN THE ANGEL, FLYING EARTHWARD,
BRUSHED THE WATERS, CALM AND COOL!

BUT THAT POOL IN OLD JUDEA
ANGELS LEFT LONG YEARS AGO,
WHEN THE NATIONS MIGHTY HEALER
STOOPED FROM BLISS TO EARTHLY WOE
NOW TO ALL THE HEAVY HEARTED
COMES HIS TENDER, LOVING PLEA:
"SEEK THE MAGIC FOUNT NO LONGER;
I WILL HEAL YOU. COME FOLLOW ME!"

"POEMS TO CONSIDER"

O GIVE ME, LORD, TO UNDERSTAND,
THY WAY TO WALK AT THY COMMAND;
AND HELP ME, LORD, EACH DAY TO BE
A REPRESENTATIVE OF THEE.

HELP ME TO GIVE, FOR EVERY FROWN,
A PLEASANT SMILE; FOR CROSS, A CROWN;
FOR SIZE, A SYMPATHETIC TEAR;
FOR BROKEN HEARTS, A WORD OF CHEER;

A KINDLY HAND TO THOSE WHO FAINT
BENEATH THE BURDEN OF COMPLAINT:
A LIFE FOR ALL CONDEMNED TO DIE,
THAT I MAY LIVE, AND YET NOT I.

OH, LIVE THINE OWN DEAR LIFE IN ME,
THAT I MAY REPRESENT BUT THEE!

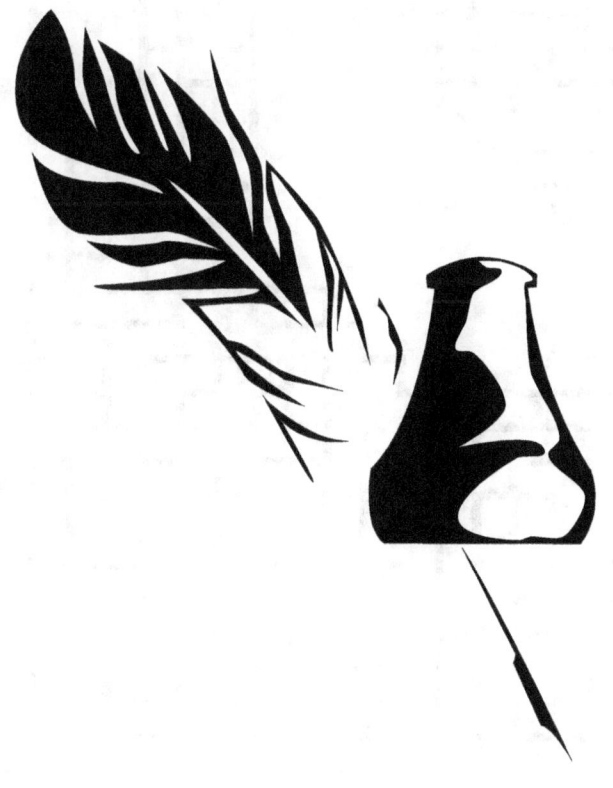

"HARMONY IN MAZES"

SEEK AND FIND YOUR WAY THROUGH THE MAZE BELOW

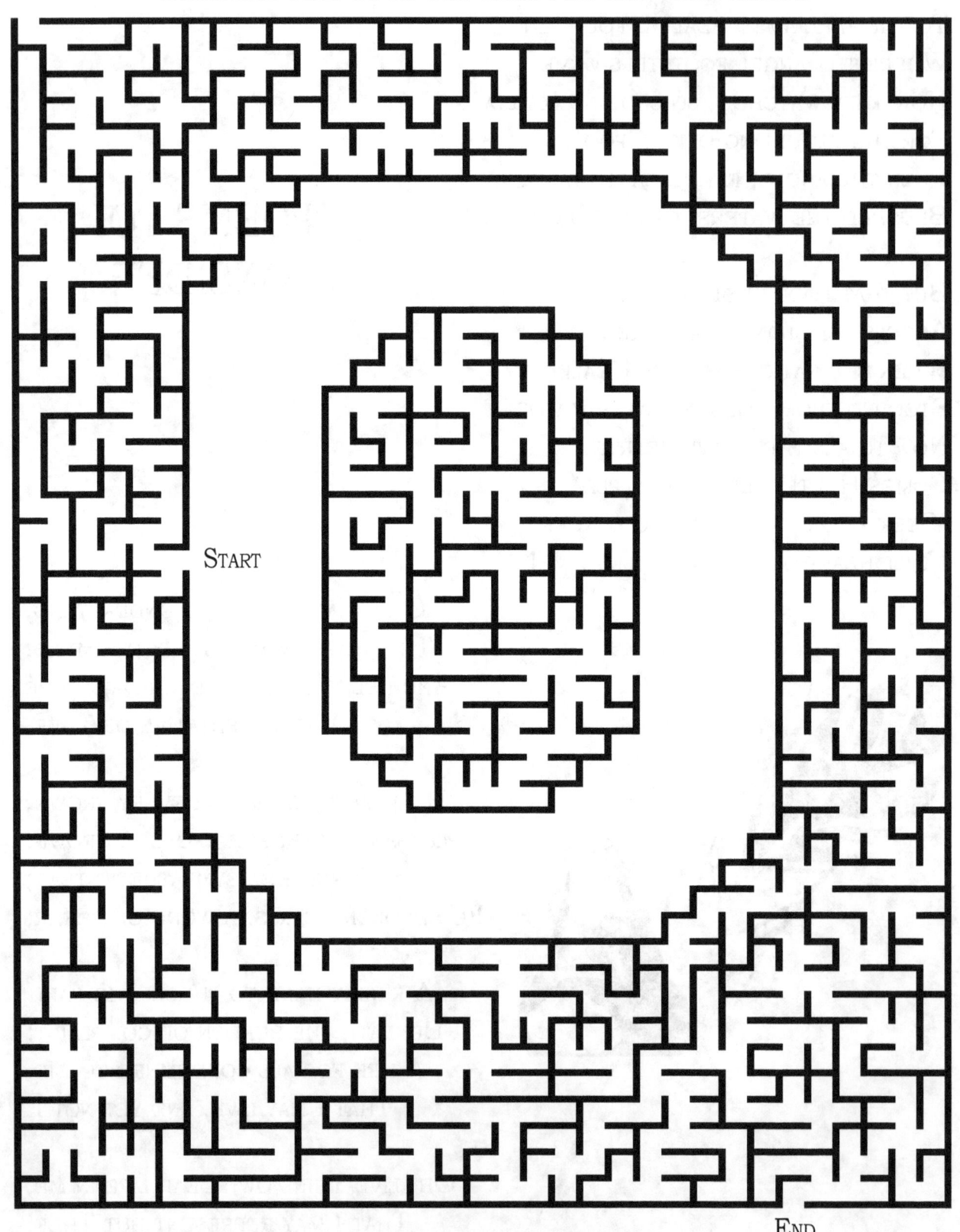

START

END

SEE HOW MANY WORDS
YOU CAN RHYME WITH

HEAVEN

"O GIVE THANKS UNTO THE GOD OF HEAVEN: FOR HIS MERCY ENDURETH FOR EVER."
~ PSALM 136:26

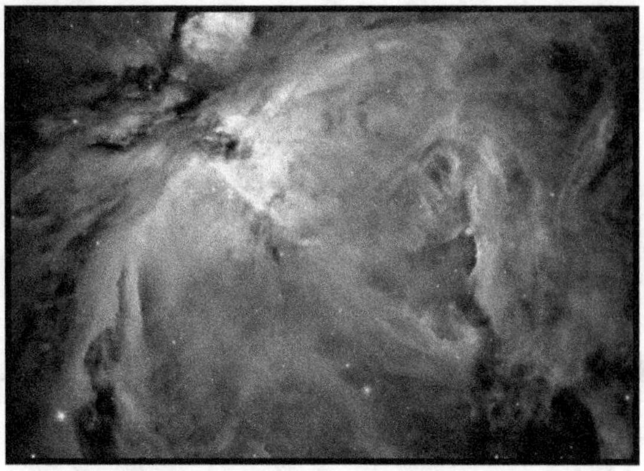

_____

_____

_____

_____   _____

_____   _____

_____   _____

_____   _____

SECRET MESSAGE 1

A	B	C	D	E	F	G	H	I	J	K	L	M	N	O	P	Q	R	S	T	U	V	W	X	Y	Z
9	4	15	21	26	10	18	5	16	1	13	6	23	8	2	14	24	11	3	17	25	7	19	12	20	22

USE THE ABOVE KEYS TO DECODE THE MESSAGE BELOW

3 14 26 9 13 16 8 18   17 2

20 2 25 11 3 26 6 7 26 3   16 8

14 3 9 6 23 3   9 8 21

5 20 23 8 3   9 8 21

3 14 16 11 16 17 25 9 6

3 2 8 18 3 ,   3 16 8 18 16 8 18

9 8 21   23 9 13 16 8 18

23 26 6 2 21 20   16 8

20 2 25 11   5 26 9 11 17   17 2

17 5 26   6 2 11 21 .

WHERE IS THIS TEXT FOUND: _____

SECRET MESSAGE 1: ANSWERS FOUND ON PAGE 34

SING A SONG
FIND THESE WORDS IN THE FOREST OF LETTERS

```
C H O I R D O V P F M F M E J I S M W V R N Q F M
P V D R H C V V W K M G F E E C I O F V O C K I S
S V M T H B T U N E L J V A S Q N A N S P I K U T
A A K E D Y M F W Y P R L L M K G J H P A R C K Y
L L C P L F T O S C H O T V W F I R T C P O E E X
M T U E B O B H T S Y S G D F A N T Q B M Z K Z J
S O E D I K D U M N M J Y P V C G Q I C M S S X N
W Y E F S E K Y A G N Q I S J O M M N M S A B Z E
K I O I B O J F C L N A C I Q M H H S R C V W N Z
M S Z F G C P O C D W I W N J P B Q T J B S D Q Z
J M E K U H B R W L R Y Z F C O I L R G Q C A G M
L Q N R R O A E A Y R F Y Z P S X E U D J C L X T
S C O Z U J P S L N K K I J R I F S M M A J A C G
U D T H A R M O N Y O M S W A T P O E R U A X N E
X S E O V R T U H Y K S W E I I L U N J E S O F N
O Q V I Y B K E I W A N Y Q S O R N T O T S I X G
E M U V B S K Z B B C Y Y B E N V D W R T Y P C A
```

MUSIC	LYRICS	PSALMS	RHYTHM
NOTE	MELODY	BASS	PRAISE
COMPOSITION	HYMN	SONG	SOPRANO
SINGING	SOUND	INSTRUMENT	HARMONY
VOICE	TUNE	ALTO	CHOIR

WORD SEARCH 2: ANSWERS FOUND ON PAGE 36

STRING, WIND, BRASS OR PERCUSSION?

PLEASE LABEL WHICH INSTRUMENT IS STRING, WIND, BRASS OR PERCUSSION.

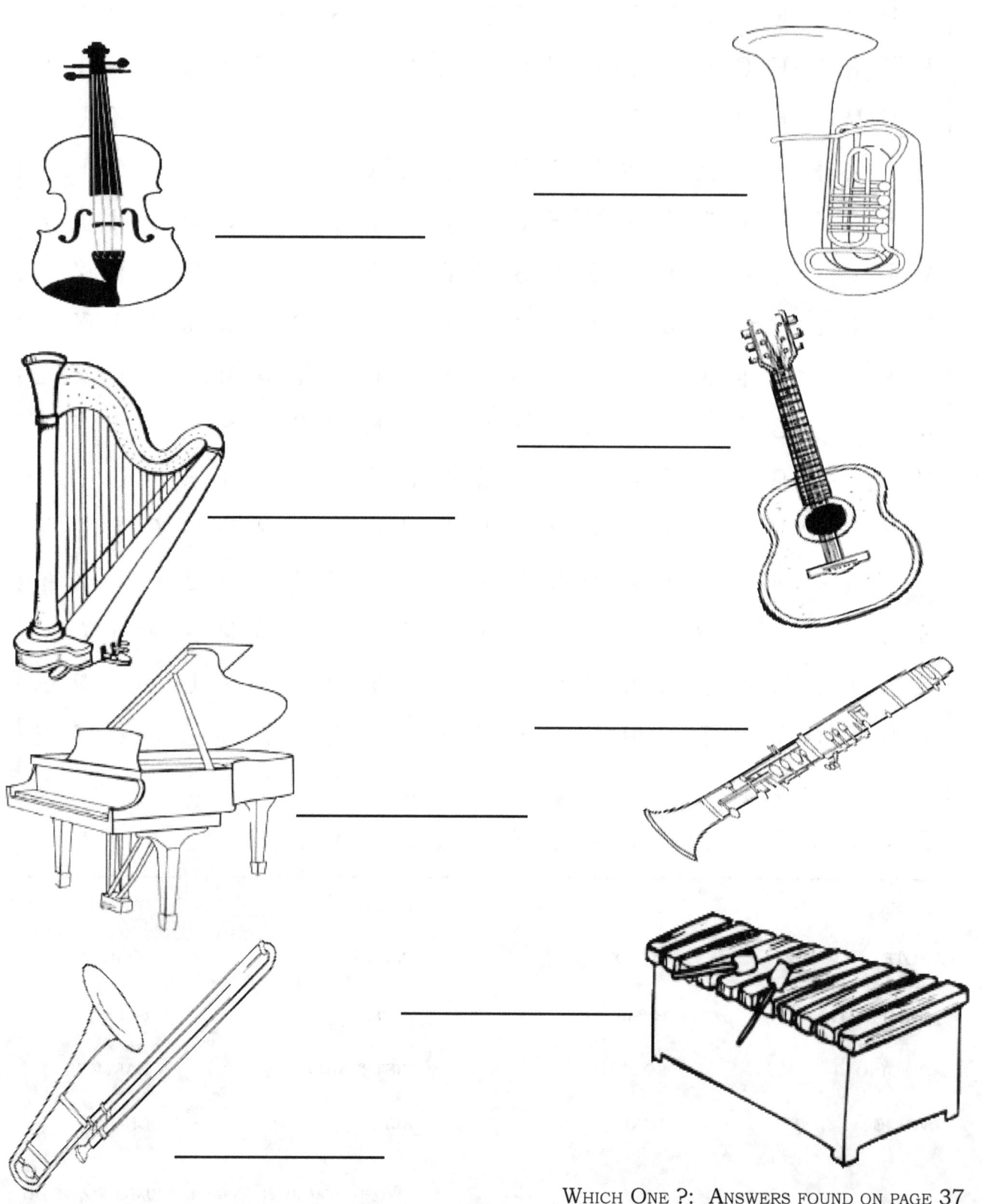

WHICH ONE ?: ANSWERS FOUND ON PAGE 37

SONGS TO SING
CROSSWORD PUZZLE 2

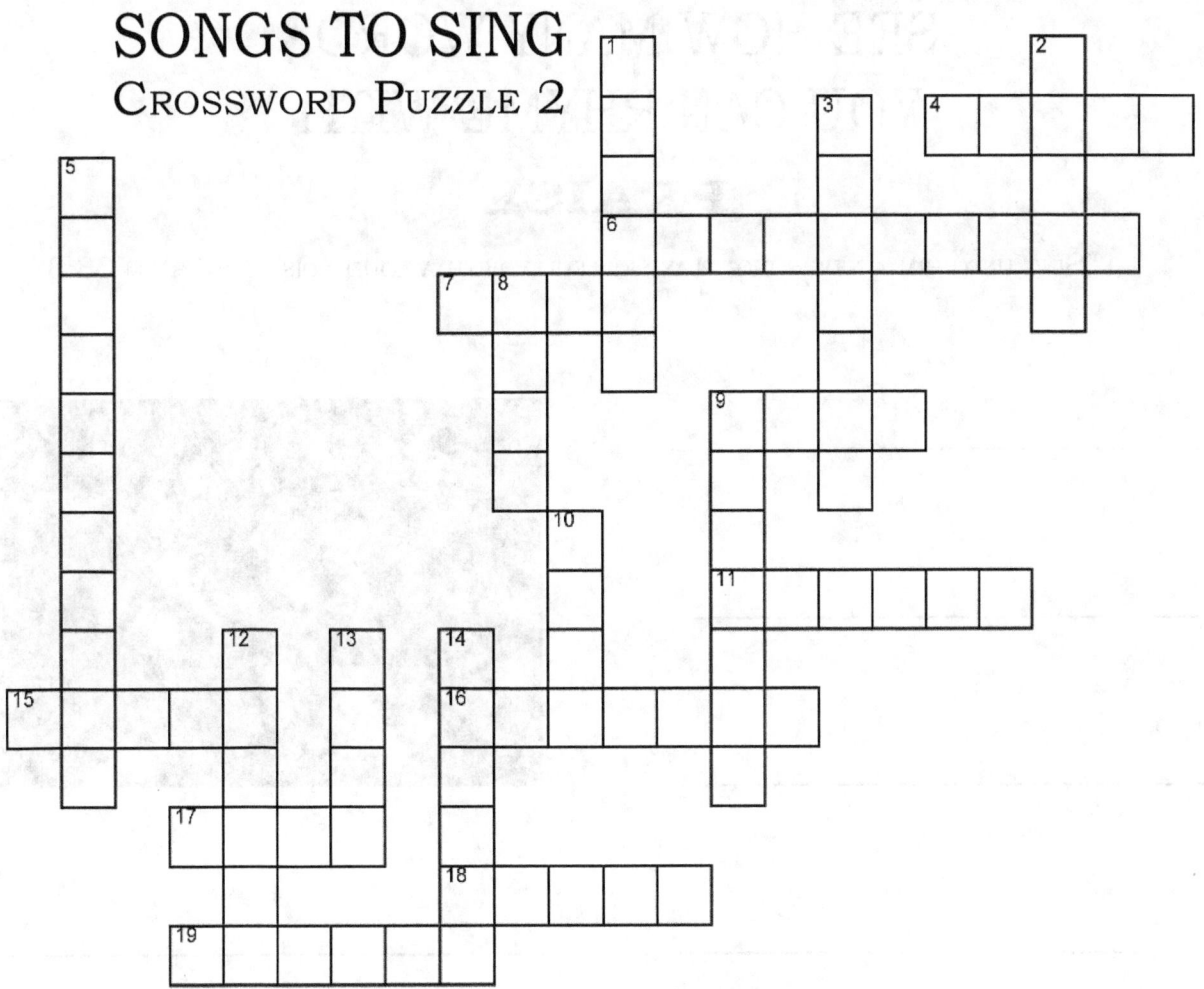

ACROSS

4. A ORGANIZED COLLECTION OF SINGERS, ESPECIALLY ONE PERFORMING CHURCH MUSIC OR SINGING IN A CHURCH.

6. A DEVICE FOR PLAYING OR PRODUCING MUSIC.

7. TO SOUND IN A DEEP TONE.

9. A BRIEF COMPOSITION WRITTEN OR ADAPTED FOR SINGING.

11. IN MUSIC, THE VARIETY IN THE MOVEMENT AS TO QUICKNESS OR SLOWNESS OR LENGTH AND SHORTNESS OF THE NOTES.

15. SOUND OR AUDIBLE NOISE UTTERED BY THE MOUTH.

16. TO UTTER A SERIES OF WORDS OR SOUNDS IN MUSICAL TONES.

17. A TONE OF DEFINITE PITCH. SYMBOL FOR A TONE INDICATING PITCH BY ITS POSITION OF THE STAFF AND DURATION BY ITS SHAPE.

18. THE ART OF ARRANGING SOUNDS IN TIME SO AS TO PRODUCE A CONTINUOUS, UNIFIED, AND EVOCATIVE COMPOSITION, AS THROUGH MELODY, HARMONY, RHYTHM, AND TIMBRE.

19. WORDS PUT TOGETHER FOR A POEM OR SONG.

DOWN

1. TO EXALT IN WORDS OR SONG; TO MAGNIFY; TO GLORIFY ON ACCOUNT OF PERFECTIONS OR EXCELLENT WORKS.

2. TO MAKE A NOISE. VIBRATIONS THAT STRIKE THE ORGANS OF HEARING.

3. A COMBINATION OF SOUNDS CONSIDERED PLEASING TO THE EAR.

5. IN MUSIC, THE ACT OR ART OF FORMING TUNES. A TUNE, SONG, ANTHEM, OR OTHER MUSICAL PIECE.

8. A LOW FEMALE SINGING VOICE.

9. THE HIGHEST SINGING VOICE OF A WOMAN OR YOUNG BOY.

10. A SHORT POEM COMPOSED FOR RELIGIOUS SERVICE. A SONG OF PRAISE OR THANKSGIVING TO GOD.

12. A PLEASING SUCCESSION OR ARRANGEMENT OF SOUNDS.

13. TO SING WITH MELODY OR HARMONY. A SONG.

14. SACRED SONGS OR HYMNS; SONGS COMPOSED ON A DIVINE SUBJECT AND IN PRAISE OF GOD.

CROSSWORD PUZZLE 2: ANSWERS FOUND ON PAGE 35

SEE HOW MANY WORDS
YOU CAN RHYME WITH

PRAISE

"SING UNTO HIM A NEW SONG; PLAY SKILLFULLY WITH A LOUD NOISE." ~ PSALM 33:3

_____

_____

_____   _____

_____   _____

_____   _____

_____   _____

FILL IN THE BLANK
COMMIT THESE VERSES OF SCRIPTURE TO MEMORY

ALSO I WILL _____ HIM MY _____, HIGHER THAN THE _____ OF THE _____.
~ PSALM 89:27

I WILL MAKE _____ OF _____ AND _____ TO THEM THAT _____ ME: BEHOLD
PHILISTIA, AND _____, WITH _____; THIS MAN WAS _____ THERE. ~ PSALM 87:4

THOU DIDST _____ THE SEA BY THY _____: THOU _____ THE _____ OF THE
_____ IN THE WATERS. ~ PSALM 74:13

_____ US THY MERCY, O LORD, AND _____ US THY _____. ~ PSALM 85:7

BEHOLD, HE _____ THE _____, THAT THE _____ GUSHED OUT, AND THE _____
OVERFLOWED; CAN HE GIVE _____ ALSO? CAN HE _____ FLESH FOR HIS _____?
~ PSALM 78:20

WHO _____ THROUGH THE _____ OF _____ MAKE IT A _____; THE _____ ALSO
FILLETH THE _____. ~ PSALM 84:6

FOR IN THE _____ OF THE LORD THERE IS A _____, AND THE _____ IS _____; IT IS FULL OF
MIXTURE; AND HE _____ OUT OF THE SAME: BUT THE _____ THEREOF, ALL THE _____
OF THE _____ SHALL _____ THEM OUT, AND _____ THEM. ~ PSALM 75:8

AND THE _____ WHICH THY _____ HAND HATH _____, AND THE _____ THAT
THOU MADEST _____ FOR THYSELF. ~ PSALM 80:15

I AM _____ AND READY TO DIE FROM MY _____ UP: WHILE I _____ THY _____
I AM _____. ~ PSALM 88:15

SONGS TO SING
CROSSWORD PUZZLE 3
"FIND THE WORD THAT RHYMES WITH THE CAPITALIZED WORDS"

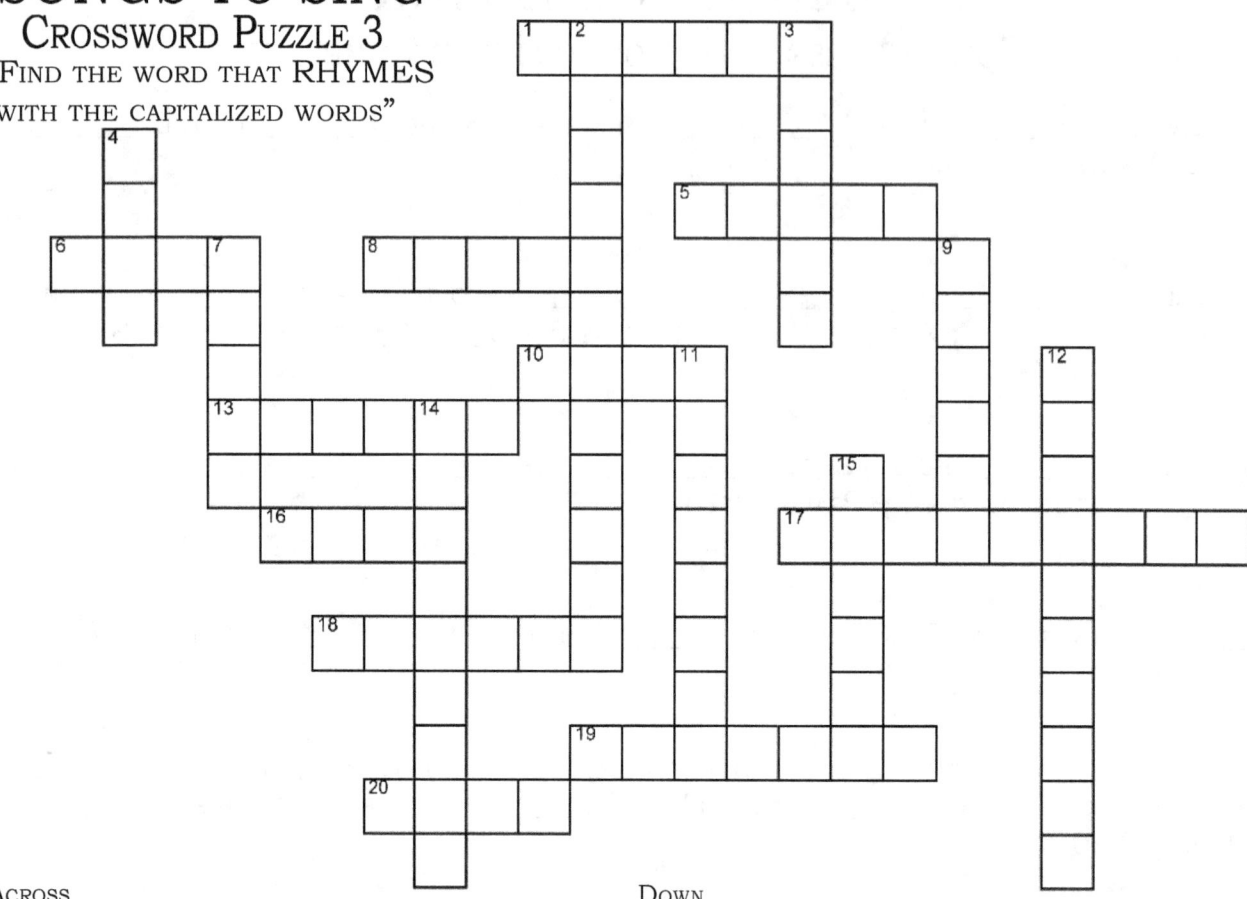

ACROSS

1. THE PRIEST WORE ANOTHER LAYER OF CLOTHES UNDER HIS OUTER GARMENTS. (1 PETER 4:7)

5. THE SPIRIT OF GOD RESTED ON THE MERCY SEAT. (JOHN 12:24)

6. ISRAEL DURING THE TIME OF JOSHUA HAD AN ACHAN IN THE CAMP. (PSALM 119:105)

8. MAN WILL NEITHER KNOW THE DAY NOR THE HOUR WHEN CHRIST COMETH. (2 TIMOTHY 1:7)

10. CHRIST CAME TO SEEK AND SAVE THE LOST. (MATTHEW 11:29)

13. HE PAID AN INFINITE PRICE. (MATTHEW 16:16)

16. ISAIAH HAD A PIECE OF COAL LAID UPON HIS MOUTH. (MATTHEW 16:26)

17. AFTER CROSSING THE RED SEA, GOD WAS DISPLEASED WITH THE FESTIVITY OF THE ISRAELITES. (2 CORINTHIANS 10:5)

18. THE PASSOVER BREAD IS MADE WITHOUT LEAVEN. (GENESIS 7:11)

19. CHRIST PROMISES US LIFE EVERLASTING IF WE OBEY HIM. (JOEL 2:12)

20. NOAH RELEASED A DOVE TO SEARCH FOR DRY LAND AFTER THE FLOOD. (1 JOHN 5:3)

DOWN

2. WE ARE TO STRIVE FOR THE PERFECTION OF CHRIST'S CHARACTER. (JOHN 5:29)

3. JOSEPH WAS KNOWN AS THE DREAMER OF DREAMS. (JEREMIAH 15:21)

4. THE 8TH COMMANDMENT TELLS US THAT WE SHOULD NOT STEAL. (LUKE 4:18)

7. AARON'S POSITION IN THE SANCTUARY WAS HIGH PRIEST. (GALATIANS 5:22,23)

9. JACOB, WHEN WRESTLING THE ANGEL, HAD HIS THIGH PUSHED OUT OF JOINT. (MARK 16:1)

11. CHRIST HEALED MANY THAT SUFFERED FROM BLINDNESS. (COLOSSIANS 3:12-14)

12. BAPTISM BY WATER IS ALSO CALLED IMMERSION. (ACTS 15:3)

14. AND LEAD US NOT, INTO TEMPTATION. (PSALM 51:12)

15. CHRIST SACRIFICED HIS LIFE TO PARDON OUR SINS. (GENESIS 2:8)

CROSSWORD PUZZLE 3: ANSWERS FOUND ON PAGE 35

SECRET MESSAGE 2

A	B	C	D	E	F	G	H	I	J	K	L	M	N	O	P	Q	R	S	T	U	V	W	X	Y	Z
24	8	16	1	15	26	10	3	17	4	13	23	14	7	18	22	6	19	12	25	11	20	2	9	21	5

USE THE ABOVE KEYS TO DECODE THE MESSAGE BELOW

__17__   __2__ __17__ __23__ __23__   __12__ __17__ __7__ __10__   __24__

__7__ __15__ __2__   __12__ __18__ __7__ __10__   __11__ __7__ __25__ __18__

__25__ __3__ __15__ __15__ ,   __18__   __10__ __18__ __1__ ;

__11__ __22__ __18__ __7__   __24__

__22__ __12__ __24__ __23__ __25__ __15__ __19__ __21__   __24__ __7__ __1__

__24__ __7__   __17__ __7__ __12__ __25__ __19__ __11__ __14__ __15__ __7__ __25__

__18__ __26__   __25__ __15__ __7__   __12__ __25__ __19__ __17__ __7__ __10__ __12__

__2__ __17__ __23__ __23__   __17__   __12__ __17__ __7__ __10__

__22__ __19__ __24__ __17__ __12__ __15__ __12__   __11__ __7__ __25__ __18__

__25__ __3__ __15__ __15__ .

WHERE IS THIS TEXT FOUND: _____

SECRET MESSAGE 2: ANSWERS FOUND ON PAGE 34

"HARMONY IN MAZES"

SEEK AND FIND YOUR WAY THROUGH THE MAZE BELOW

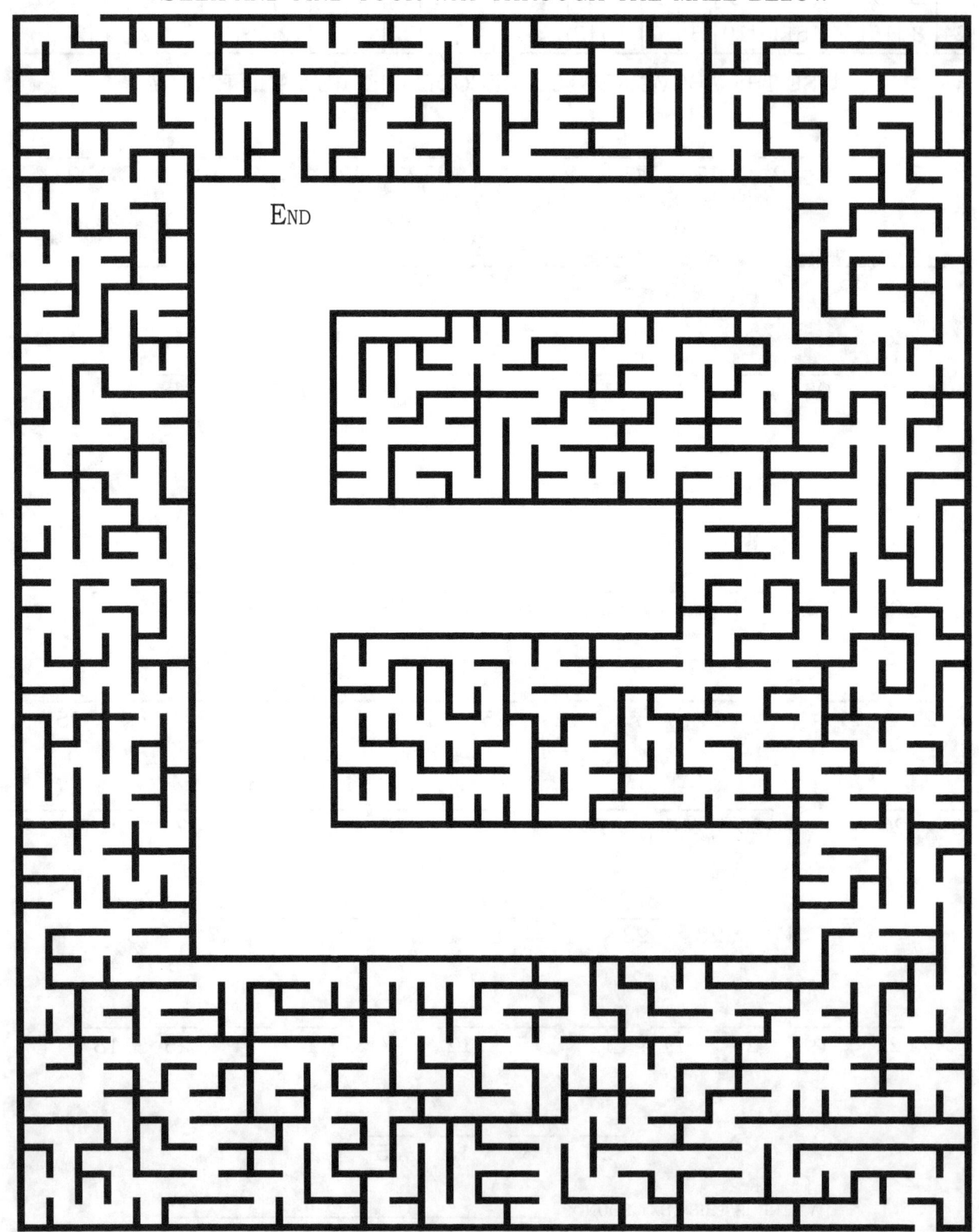

END

START

SCRIPTURE SONGS 4 LEARNING

VERSE 1:

O GIVE THANKS
GIVE THANKS UNTO THE LORD;
FOR HE IS GOOD:
AND HIS MERCY ENDURETH FOR EVER.
THE LORD IS MY STRENGTH, AND MY SONG
AND BECOME MY SALVATION.

CHORUS:

NOW, LET ISRAEL NOW SAY,
HIS MERCY ENDURETH FOR EVER.
LET THE HOUSE OF AARON SAY,
HIS MERCY ENDURETH FOR EVER.
LET THEM THAT FEARETH THE LORD SAY,
HIS MERCY ENDURETH FOR EVER.
HE'S MY STRENGTH, AND MY SONG
AND MY SALVATION.

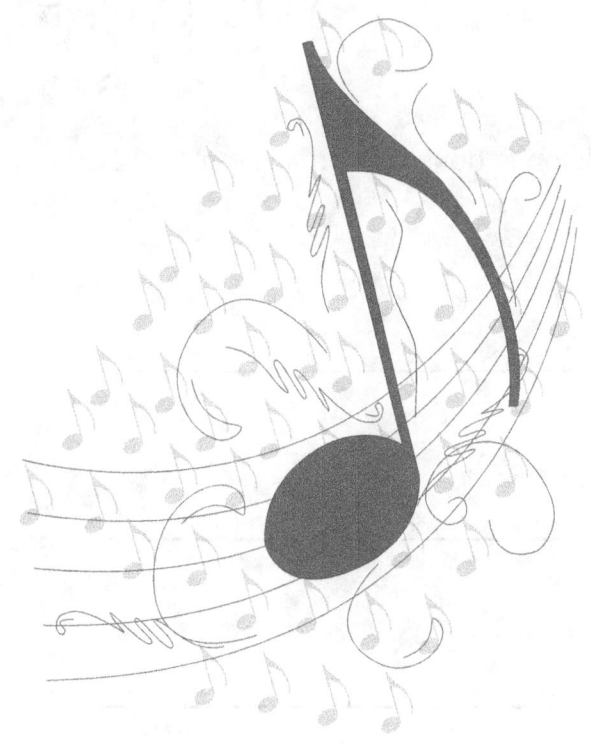

VERSE 2:

IT IS BETTER TO TRUST THE LORD,
THAN TO TRUST IN MAN.
IT IS BETTER TO TRUST THE LORD,
THAN TO TRUST IN PRINCES.
OPEN UP TO ME THE GATES OF RIGHTEOUSNESS:
I WILL GO UNTO THEM, AND PRAISE THE LORD:

CHORUS:

VERSE 1:

CHORUS:

PSALM 118:1-4, 8, 9, 14, 19

THE LORD THY GOD IN THE MIDST OF THEE IS
MIGHTY,
MIGHTY.
HE WILL SAVE,
HE'LL REJOICE OVER THEE WITH JOY;
WITH JOY.
HE WILL REST IN HIS LOVE,
HE WILL JOY OVER THEE WITH SINGING.
THE LORD THY GOD IN THE MIDST OF THEE IS
MIGHTY,
MIGHTY,
SO MIGHTY.

(REPEAT: HIGHER NOTE)

ZEPHANIAH 3:17

SEE HOW MANY WORDS
YOU CAN RHYME WITH
SOUND

"GOD IS GONE UP WITH A SHOUT, THE LORD WITH THE SOUND OF A TRUMPET." ~ PSALM 47:5

BIBLE TRIVIA 2: "PSALMS"

1. THE HEADS OF WHAT WERE BROKEN IN THE WATER ACCORDING TO PSALM 74:13 (KJV)?

A) WHALES   B) LIONS   C) DRAGONS   D) UNICORNS

2. WHAT IS RED IN PSALM 75:8?

A) BLOOD   B) WINE   C) TONGUE   D) OCEAN

3. IN PSALM 78 THE PSALMIST REMINDS US OF GOD'S POWER IN EGYPT. WHAT DOES HE SAY CAME FROM A ROCK?

A) STONES   B) WATER   C) APPLE JUICE   D) BLOOD

4. ACCORDING TO PSALM 80:15, WHAT DID THE RIGHT HAND PLANT?

A) VINEYARD   B) CORN   C) RICE   D) WHEAT

5. WHAT IS THE NAME OF THE VALLEY MENTIONED IN PSALM 84:6?

A) DEATH   B) BACA   C) SILICON   D) TENNESSEE

6. PSALM 85 TALKS ABOUT MERCY. WHAT IS MERCY?

A) GOD PUNISHING US FOR OUR SINS
B) GOD GRANTING US WHAT WE DON'T DESERVE
C) GOD GIVING US TWO EYES
D) WHAT YOU SAY WHEN YOU WANT THE OTHER PERSON TO STOP SQUEEZING YOUR HAND

7. THE PSALMIST IN CHAPTER 87 MENTIONS WHERE HE WAS BORN. WHERE IS IT?

A) PERSIA   B) CANADA   C) ISRAEL   D) ETHIOPIA

8. WHAT DOES DAVID SAY HE IS READY TO DO IN PSALM 88:15?

A) DANCE   B) DIE   C) SLEEP   D) PARTY

9. WHO CAN STILL THE WAVES OF THE SEA?

ANSWER:

10. PSALM 89:27 IS CONSIDERED TO PREDICT WHOSE BIRTH?

A) JOHN   B) PAUL   C) PETER   D) JESUS

BIBLE TRIVIA 2: ANSWERS FOUND ON PAGE 34

SECRET MESSAGE 3

A	B	C	D	E	F	G	H	I	J	K	L	M	N	O	P	Q	R	S	T	U	V	W	X	Y	Z
12	22	4	17	3	14	24	16	5	18	1	11	2	21	6	10	20	7	26	13	25	8	15	23	9	19

USE THE ABOVE KEYS TO DECODE THE MESSAGE BELOW

12 21 17   2 5 7 5 12 2   13 16 3

10 7 6 10 16 3 13 3 26 26 ,   13 16 3

26 5 26 13 3 7   6 14   12 12 7 6 21 ,

13 6 6 1   12   13 5 2 22 7 3 11

5 21   16 3 7   16 12 21 17 ;   12 21 17

12 11 11   13 16 3   15 6 2 3 21

15 3 21 13   6 25 13   12 14 13 3 7

16 3 7   15 5 13 16   13 5 2 22 7 3 11 26

12 21 17   15 5 13 16   17 12 21 4 3 26 .

WHERE IS THIS TEXT FOUND? _____

RHYMING TIME

FIND THESE WORDS IN THE FOREST OF LETTERS

```
W H V K F B H I V W U M F P E V D Z T M Z W J P C
Y E U I B R B I R E J E O S Y S S E I G C H M U N
N A P N A N S S M K X E B T L F W M O Q Q E F G F
V L E D D O Z O U G V K I M O M H P V N K A M R Q
Y F A N Z A G O U P C V E P I S E O O E F T J E R
Y A C E P A P F Z L I E Q V G V T I M U N M D S S
E S E S V E Y P R T D D H J O X T P B P N M Z U U
M T C S F V S Q P E X Z G L H A U C P T U R C R M
G I A Y O H C A R D U T X A V B Z Y O Y U W Z R H
K N Y J I K C P K I K C G L R B S Z W D A N P E I
J G C B Q H Y V M D H Q A I D D U K E N N C R C E
C O N V E R S I O N L S H Q T T E O R R O W A T Q
O G M O T W G C U G A X A S Z W H N Q Z I M Y I Q
P B E W W O H K K R M U I D F X N B X Z N H E O W
X P W I P H E M V K P R E T B C V B V C T P R N X
H H E A V E N H D A H Q Z K Y L B U P F M D F N B
A E U R W S A G V C J L S C B A S D P I R U N V R
```

CHRIST	SALVATION	HEAVEN	PRAYER
LOVE	PEACE	KINDNESS	MEEK
GARDEN	HEAL	LAMP	FASTING
WHEAT	SOUL	REDEEM	CAPTIVITY
ANOINT	RESURRECTION	CONVERSION	POWER

WORD SEARCH 3: ANSWERS FOUND ON PAGE 36

SEE HOW MANY WORDS
YOU CAN RHYME WITH

PERFECTION

"TRULY THE LIGHT IS SWEET, AND A PLEASANT THING IT IS FOR THE EYES TO BEHOLD THE SUN." ~ ECCLESIASTES 11:7

_____

_____

_____

_____   _____

_____   _____

_____   _____

_____   _____

UNSCRAMBLE EXERCISE
UNSCRAMBLE THE MUSICAL WORDS BELOW

DOYELM: _____

OOBERTMN: _____

RYMHNAO: _____

YICRL: _____

UEISNNTMRT: _____

NOAPROS: _____

CNEPSORUIS: _____

EOYTPR: _____

EOMPT: _____

CHESTRROA: _____

UCNTORCDO: _____

REESV: _____

ZSAATN: _____

ANRFEIR: _____

HCSDOHRPAIR: _____

SUMCI: _____

UNSCRAMBLE EXERCISE: ANSWERS FOUND ON PAGE 37

COLORING ACTIVITY

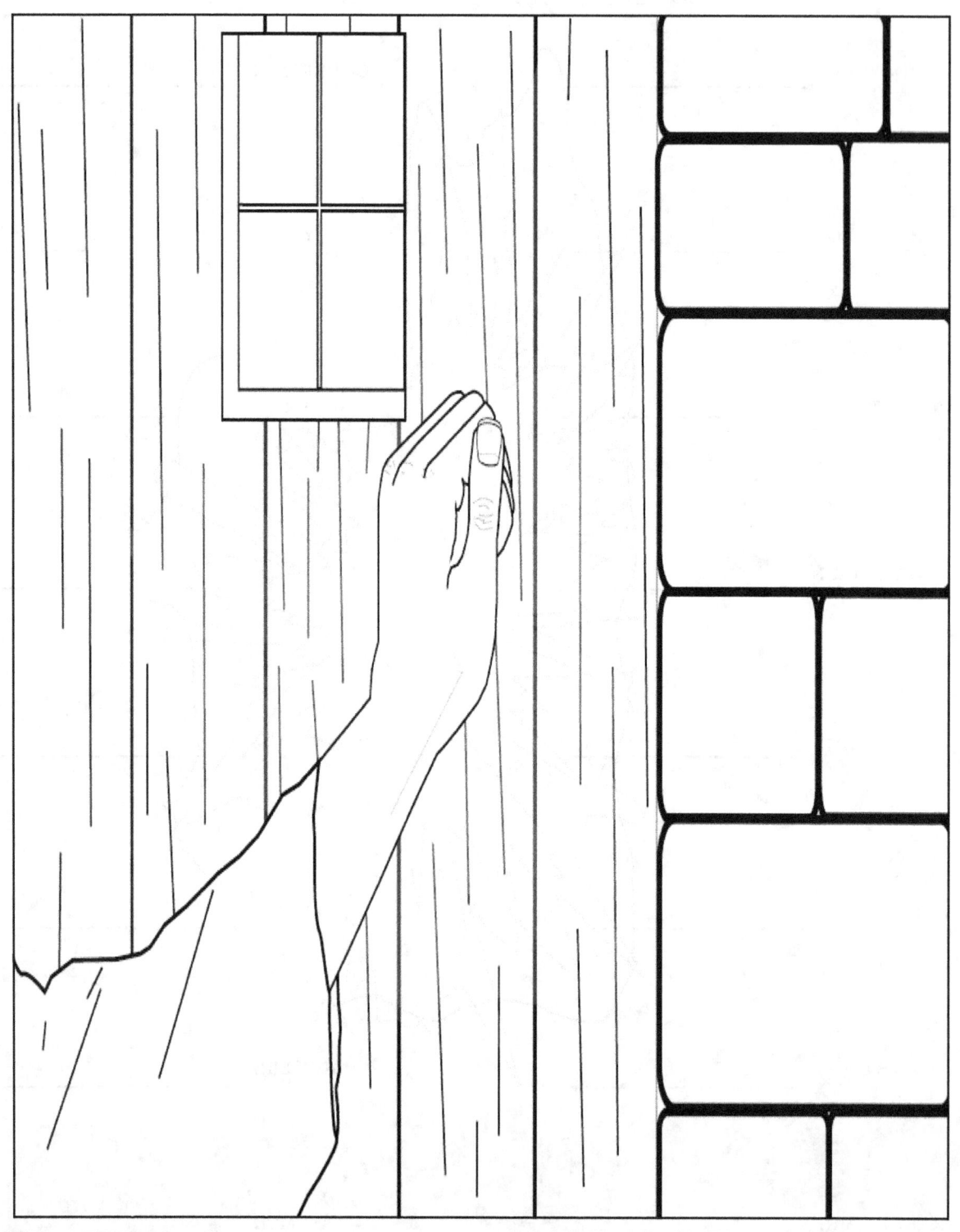

THE KNOCK

TO BE...... OR NOT TO BE
FIND THE WORDS BELOW IN THE FOREST OF LETTERS

```
K P W G R E F R A I N X L W K T S P E A K E R X M
M L H V O J R O R P Y B O O U W R T H E M E I O O
U W I Q U Y R X P J A L I D I I Z Q K G T O I H N
H R K M C G S F N H O B G V E R S E Q W R E A E O
X N J I E U R R N B P D S K Y C M M U X T I K E L
T H R J C R M U Z Q Q V M E P U J U I I R D L Y O
M D Q V B G I H P L I W J X Q C O O C O H B C B G
P S Q P K P T C N M O U T P P V P E D C A D K S U
Q P G Y I E O P K L O K H R M Y R N E L E L P N E
Y J H L N J D E F Y K P T E Q X W E L H Z D V R Q
V W U N O O A L M C P W L S E Q P Y S E X L F H Z
R F O F R E E V E R S E D S Y S S R S I M O J Y G
P S Z T N X K A J Y F A T I I Q E P I C W E D M P
N A Z D B Z U K W L L N Y O H A I K U Z U A S E Z
Q W K S B F I J R L R A T N Y S Q Z Q M F I D W G
F B J W F O Z L A Z L V S J E Z E G Y D O H B D M
U P Y X J R C B E H L B S J M T E G D F Y L L G H
```

POEM	RHYME	LIMERICK	SONNET
ODE	FLOW	MONOLOGUE	SPEECH
VERSE	BALLAD	HAIKU	EPIC
FREE VERSE	SPEAKER	RECITE	EXPRESSION
THEME	REFRAIN	SYLLABLE	

WORD SEARCH 4: ANSWERS FOUND ON PAGE 36

SECRET MESSAGE 4

A	B	C	D	E	F	G	H	I	J	K	L	M	N	O	P	Q	R	S	T	U	V	W	X	Y	Z
17	6	20	2	21	24	13	4	14	8	22	1	26	7	18	25	9	3	15	23	5	16	10	19	11	12

USE THE ABOVE KEYS TO DECODE THE MESSAGE BELOW

I WILL ALSO

PRAISE THEE WITH

THE PSALTERY EVEN

THY TRUTH, O MY

GOD: UNTO THEE WILL

I SING WITH THE

HARP, O THOU HOLY

ONE OF ISRAEL.

WHERE IS THIS TEXT FOUND: _____

SECRET MESSAGE 4: ANSWERS FOUND ON PAGE 34

SEE HOW MANY WORDS
YOU CAN RHYME WITH

MUSIC

"BEHOLD THEIR SITTING DOWN, AND THEIR RISING UP; I AM THEIR MUSICK." ~ LAMENTATIONS 3:63

_____

_____

_____   _____

_____   _____

_____   _____

_____   _____

TO BE... OR NOT TO BE
CROSSWORD PUZZLE 4

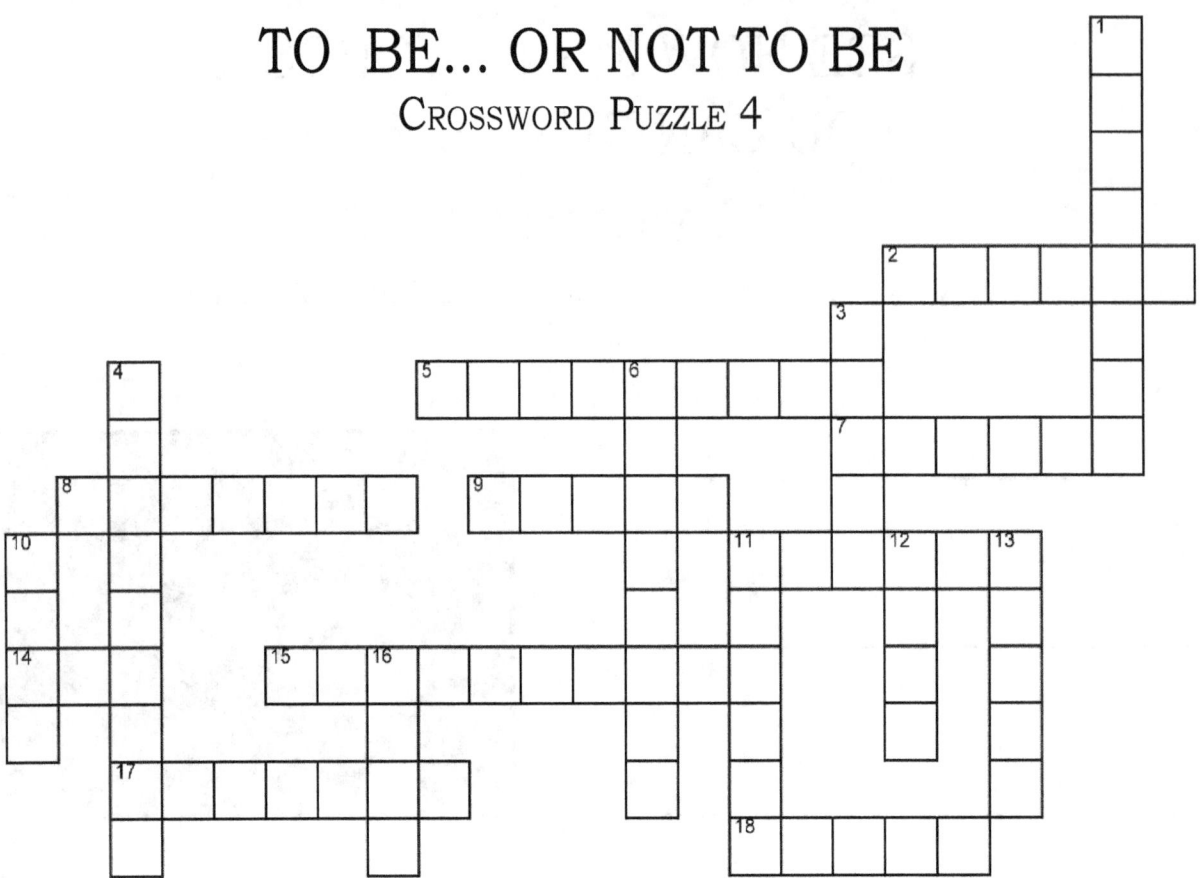

ACROSS

2. THIS IS AN OLD STYLE OF WRITING POETRY, WHICH WAS USED TO TELL STORIES.

5. A LONG SPEECH MADE BY ONE PERSON. A POEM, SONG OR SCENE COMPOSED FOR A SINGLE PERFORMER.

7. TO REPEAT OR UTTER ALOUD (SOMETHING REHEARSED OR MEMORIZED), ESPECIALLY BEFORE AN AUDIENCE.

8. A PHRASE, VERSE, OR GROUP OF VERSES REPEATED AT INTERVALS THROUGHOUT A SONG OR POEM, ESPECIALLY AT THE END OF EACH STANZA.

9. A POEM OR VERSE HAVING A REGULAR CORRESPONDENCE OF SOUNDS, ESPECIALLY AT THE ENDS OF LINES.

11. THE FACULTY OF UTTERING ARTICULATE SOUNDS OR WORDS; LANGUAGE.

14. A LYRIC POEM OF SOME LENGTH, USUALLY OF A SERIOUS OR MEDITATIVE NATURE AND HAVING AN ELEVATED STYLE AND FORMAL STANZAIC STRUCTURE.

15. THE ACT OF EXPRESSING, CONVEYING, OR REPRESENTING IN WORDS, ART, MUSIC, OR MOVEMENT.

17. A SPOKESPERSON. ONE WHO DELIVERS A PUBLIC SPEECH.

18. A SUBJECT OR TOPIC ON WHICH A PERSON WRITES OR SPEAKS.

DOWN

1. A LETTER, OR A COMBINATION OF LETTERS UTTERED TOGETHER, OR AT A SINGLE EFFORT OR IMPULSE OF THE VOICE.

3. IN POETRY, A LINE CONSISTING OF A CERTAIN NUMBER OF LONG AND SHORT SYLLABLES.

4. THIS IS A METHOD OF WRITING POETRY, WHICH DOES NOT FOLLOW ANY STRUCTURE OR STYLE.

6. A VERY WITTY POEM AND QUITE SHORT. ABOUT 5 LINES IN A STANZA.

10. TO GLIDE ALONG SMOOTHLY WITHOUT HARSHNESS.

11. A SHORT POEM OF FOURTEEN LINES, TWO STANZAS OF FOUR VERSES EACH AND TWO OF THREE EACH.

12. THIS POEM IS USUALLY A LONG AND DESCRIPTIVE ONE WHICH TELLS A STORY.

13. A JAPANESE LYRIC VERSE FORM HAVING THREE UNRHYMED LINES OF FIVE, SEVEN, AND FIVE SYLLABLES, TRADITIONALLY INVOKING AN ASPECT OF NATURE OR THE SEASONS.

16. A COMPOSITION IN WHICH THE VERSES CONSIST OF CERTAIN MEASURES, WHETHER IN BLANK VERSE OR IN RHYME.

CROSSWORD PUZZLE 4: ANSWERS FOUND ON PAGE 35

"HARMONY IN MAZES"

SEEK AND FIND YOUR WAY THROUGH THE MAZE BELOW

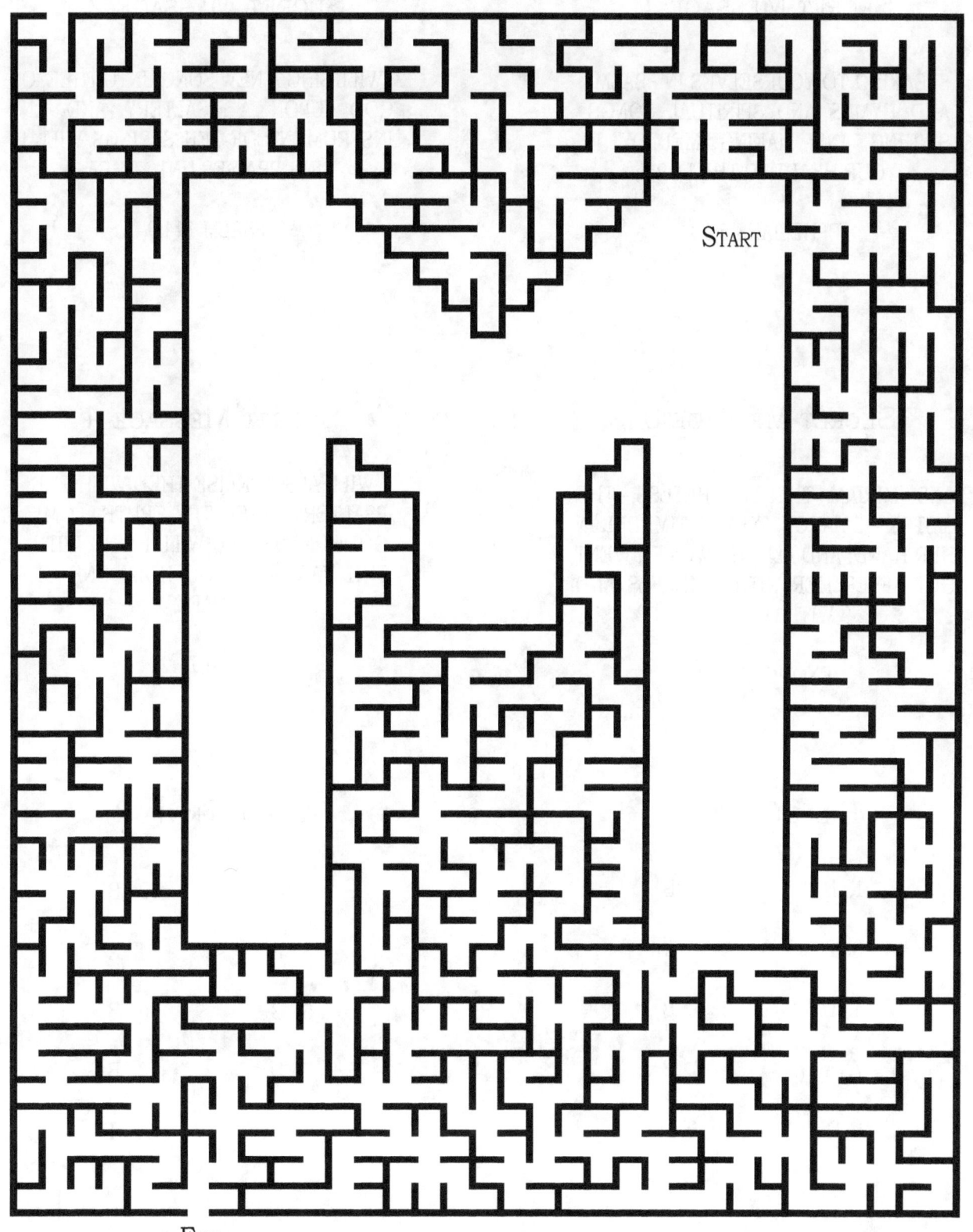

START

END

ANSWER PAGES

SECRET MESSAGE 1

SPEAKING TO YOURSELVES IN PSALMS AND HYMNS AND SPIRITUAL SONGS, SINGING AND MAKING MELODY IN YOUR HEART TO THE LORD;

EPHESIANS 5:19

SECRET MESSAGE 2

I WILL SING A NEW SONG UNTO THEE, O GOD: UPON A PSALTERY AND AN INSTRUMENT OF TEN STRINGS WILL I SING PRAISES UNTO THEE.

PSALM 144:9

SECRET MESSAGE 3

AND MIRIAM THE PROPHETESS, THE SISTER OF AARON, TOOK A TIMBREL IN HER HAND; AND ALL THE WOMEN WENT OUT AFTER HER WITH TIMBRELS AND WITH DANCES.

EXODUS 15:20

SECRET MESSAGE 4

I WILL ALSO PRAISE THEE WITH THE PSALTERY, EVEN THY TRUTH, O MY GOD: UNTO THEE WILL I SING WITH THE HARP, O THOU HOLY ONE OF ISRAEL.

PSALM 71:22

BIBLE TRIVIA 1

1. B	2. B
3. D	4. A
5. D	6. B
7. A	8. B
9. D	10. A
11. B	12. 150

BIBLE TRIVIA 2

1. C	2. B
3. B	4. A
5. B	6. B
7. D	8. B
9. GOD	10. D

CROSSWORD 1

CROSSWORD 2

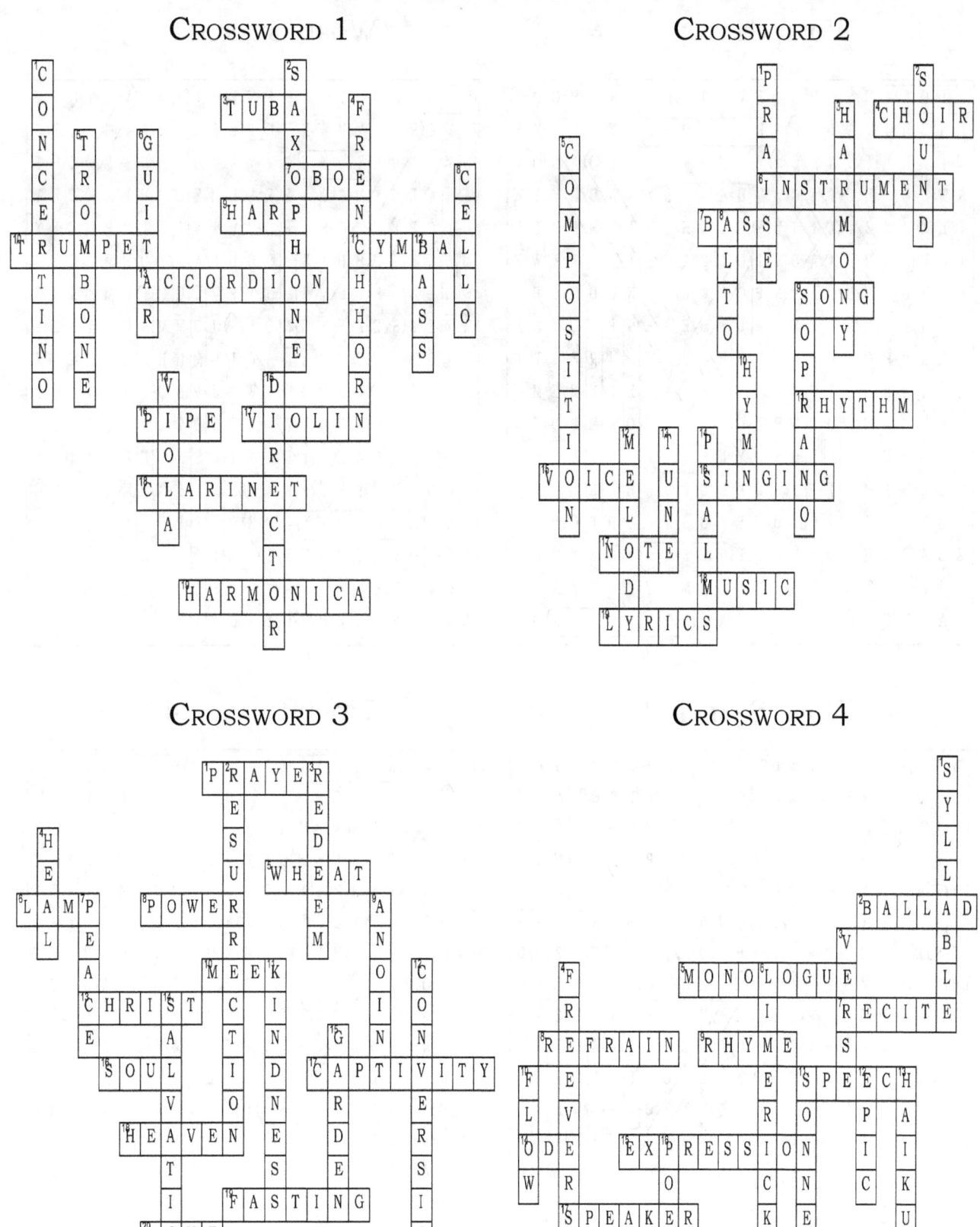

CROSSWORD 3

CROSSWORD 4

WORD SEARCH 1

WORD SEARCH 2

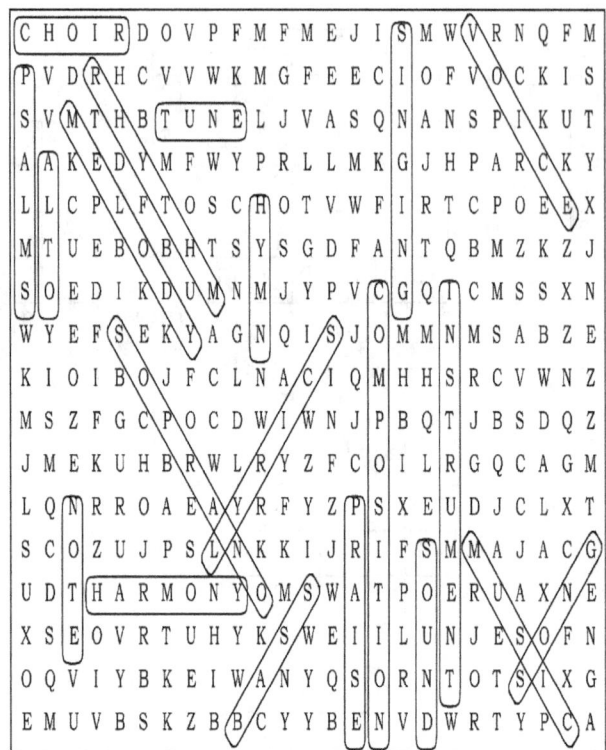

WORD SEARCH 3

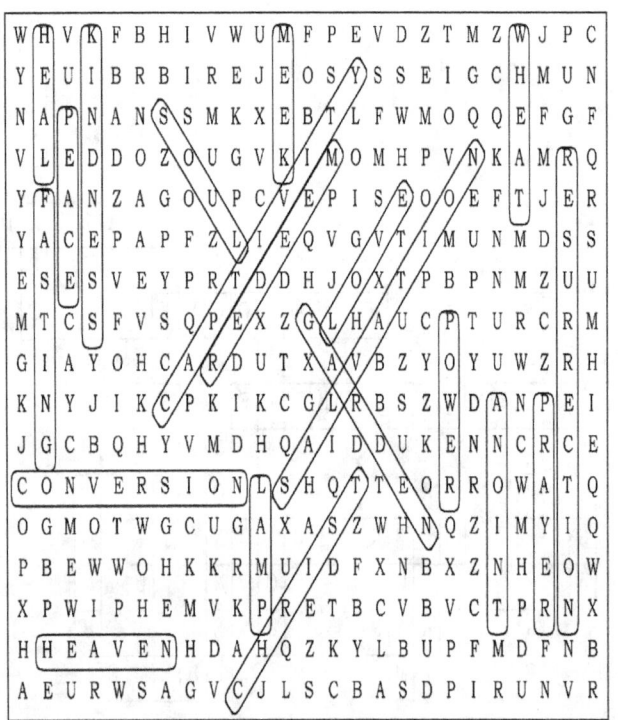

WORD SEARCH 4

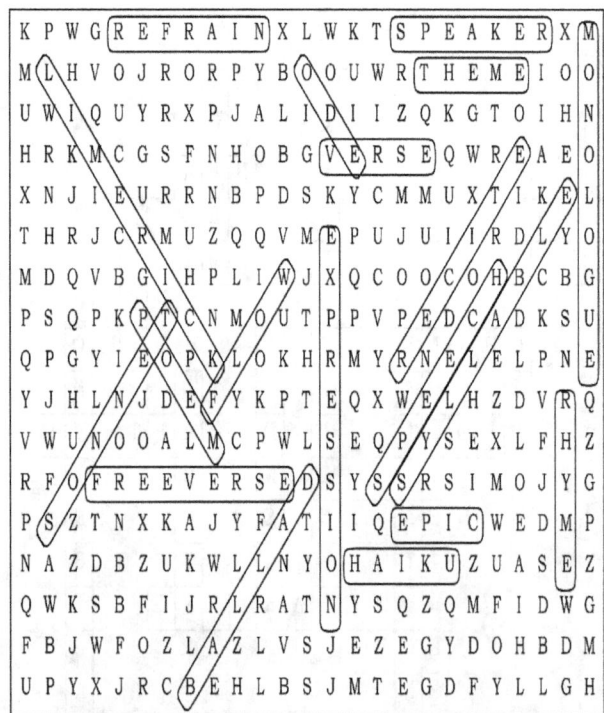

Unscramble Exercise Answers

DOYELM:	MELODY	OOBERTMN:	TROMBONE
RYMHNAO:	HARMONY	YICRL:	LYRIC
UEISNNTMRT:	INSTRUMENT	NOAPROS:	SOPRANO
CNEPSORUIS:	PERCUSSION	EOYTPR:	POETRY
EOMPT:	TEMPO	CHESTRROA:	ORCHESTRA
UCNTORCDO:	CONDUCTOR	REESV:	VERSE
ZSAATN:	STANZA	ANRFEIR:	REFRAIN
HCSDOHRPAIR:	HARPSICHORD	SUMCI:	MUSIC

Which One?

String, Wind, brass or Percussion?

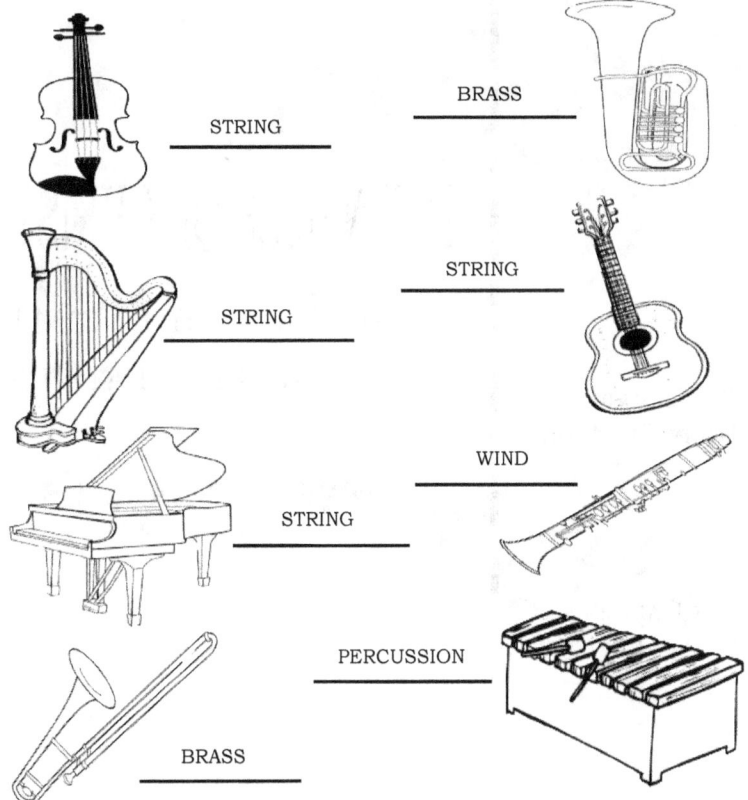

STRING

BRASS

STRING

STRING

WIND

STRING

PERCUSSION

BRASS

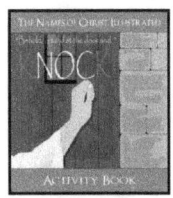 THE NOC ILLUSTRATED
ACTIVITY BOOK

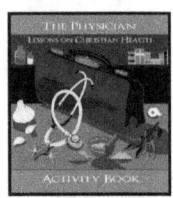 THE PHYSICIAN:
CHRISTIAN HEALTH

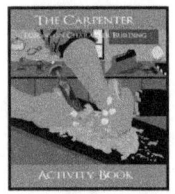 THE CARPENTER:
CHARACTER BUILDING

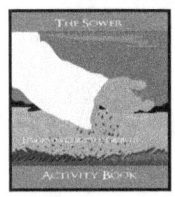 THE SOWER:
CHRISTIAN GROWTH

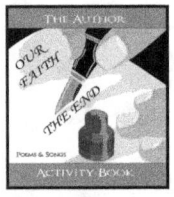 THE AUTHOR:
POEMS & SONGS

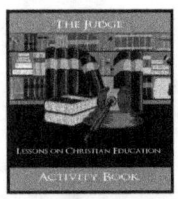 THE JUDGE:
CHRISTIAN EDUCATION

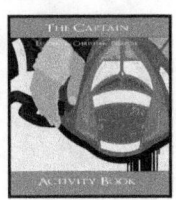 THE CAPTAIN:
CHRISTIAN PURPOSE

"PORTRAITS OF THE SAVIOUR'S
DESIRE TO ENTER HEARTS."

THIS BOOK:

THE AUTHOR
POEMS & SONGS

THE NAMES OF CHRIST ILLUSTRATED

PLEASE VISIT US ONLINE TO VIEW
MORE GREAT TITLES AT:

WWW.THENOCILLUSTRATED.COM